Real Value

New Ways to Think About
Your Time, Your Space & Your Stuff

By John Odalen

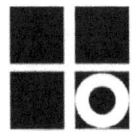

Open Door Publications

Real Value
New Ways to Think About
Your Time, Your Space & Your Stuff

Copyright © 2016 by John Odalen

ISBN: 978-0-9960985-9-5

All rights reserved.

Printed in the United States

No part of this book may be used or reproduced in any manner whatsoever without the written permission of the author except in the case of brief quotations embodied in critical articles and reviews.

Published by
Open Door Publications
2113 Stackhouse Dr.
Yardley, PA 19067
www.OpenDoorPublications.com

More Praise for *Real Value*

"John nailed it. He has taken the overwhelming task of organizing and made it simple by providing formulas for motivation and organization. It is a step by step process that he walks you through by holding your hand all the way. Whether you just can't find your keys or whether you can no longer see your floor because of all the clutter, I highly recommend you reading John's book."

Dr Dan Cruoglio
Life Adjustments Coaching, Inc

"John Odalen uses his personal and professional experience to illustrate his strategies for organizing our spaces. His plan is useful for people of all ages.

John's recommendations for finding the right place for everything are useful strategies for people starting to experience memory loss.

Older adults face particular challenges. Some find it harder to make decisions about what to keep and what to toss. Some find it more daunting to put things away, especially if they are in low or high places or down steep stairs. Clutter presents tripping hazards. Others find that they have inherited the family heirlooms and an obligation to keep them or they associate some of their things with people they have lost. Many are considering downsizing to smaller homes, so having strategies for decision making and using space well are especially helpful."

Susan Hoskins, Executive Director
Princeton Senior Resource Center

To my wonderful parents, Bill and Chris Odalen, for their encouragement and unconditional love and support.

Table of Contents

Introduction 1

How to use this book 9

Chapter 1
Change your thinking 11

Chapter 2
Change your doing 27

Chapter 3
Define the problem 35

Chapter 4
Make a plan 40

Chapter 5
Start organizing 44

Chapter 6
Specific tips 62

Chapter 7
What comes next? 91

Appendix 102

Acknowledgements 107

About the author 108

Introduction

Overwhelmed.

At some point in our lives, we have all felt overwhelmed by something: work responsibilities, family commitments, social obligations, health challenges, financial problems, the list goes on. Some things we cannot control and must do our best to cope with. And we do.

What *can* we control? Do you feel overwhelmed by all the stuff in your home? Is your home office a messy file drawer of papers? Do you want to get organized, but you do not know where to start?

This book will help you look at your stuff differently and put you on the right track to get organized and stay organized, so you can better enjoy life. We will consider the real value of our possessions. Is "real value" a dollar amount? Or the usefulness of the item? Or how it makes you feel? There are many ways to consider an item's value, none of them right or wrong. Everything is relative in terms of what is really important to you, whether it be your time, your space, or your stuff.

I wasn't always in the organizing business helping people think about their time, their space, and their stuff differently. Looking back I see how all of my previous experiences led me to my current profession as an organizer.

I started out as a computer programmer. Sounds like a very different job than an organizer, right? If you had asked me twenty years ago, I would not have seen it coming. The question is how does a computer programmer become a professional organizer?

I have always been organized. I like to have things a certain way. I find it soothing to have things in order. I sort my hanging shirts by color. If I see a bunch of shopping carts just thrown haphazardly in the corral in the grocery store parking lot, I line them all up neatly. I've been known to not just clean up the dishes after being invited to dinner, but to also straighten the pantry.

I think it must run in my family. I remember my grandfather's workshop. Every type and size of nail, screw, nut, bolt, and washer was proudly displayed in glass jars on shelves over his workbench. All of his tools were sorted and stored in foam-lined drawers. His workspace was always neat and tidy. That made sense to me. It was normal.

As a child I was very creative, always building things. In school, my favorite subject was math. It came naturally to me. I preferred facts and rules over interpretation, and hated writing—although that has since changed. I always thought I'd become an architect, but I ended up majoring in math, discovered computer science, and spent twenty years working in the research and development department of a software company. I started as a technical support representative offering telephone support to customers. I think that's where I realized I really enjoy helping people.

After the support position, I was promoted to programmer and eventually became a team leader, then manager, and eventually director. I had found my niche developing tools and defining processes to improve how the company and customers handled software maintenance. That's what it read on my resume, anyway. To the average person I fixed "software bugs." I thought of my focus as being on customer success, quality assurance, and project management. I like solving problems and working with customers; I learned to ask lots of questions, to look at the big picture, and not just the specific issue the customer was complaining about.

And then I got laid off. I spent a summer regrouping and relaxing before beginning my corporate job search. It did not go well. I had very few interviews and no job offers. I quickly learned while I was doing whatever it took to be successful with my former employer, I had not kept up with skills needed to stay competitive. My recent job experience was primarily managerial. Employers wanted managers who were also highly technical with specific industry experience I did not have. I wanted a job, but I was not excited about returning to corporate life with its pros and cons.

Meanwhile I was taking courses at my local community college in Project Management. One of my instructors told me about the Entrepreneurship class he would be teaching. I decided to enroll.

During the class I realized starting my own business might be the answer as to what I should do in the next phase of my life. The coursework helped me write my business plan and eventually launch my business.

Organizing is more than arranging items to look neat, orderly, and pretty. Any organizational system is worthless if it doesn't meet the client's needs, and if the client cannot maintain the system.

Real Value

I am careful not to project any strict standards on my clients. Sometimes good enough is good enough. Perfectionism is often the downfall of organization. I know. I understand the feeling of being overwhelmed. In wanting something to be perfect, I may find myself leaving a project unfinished until I can devote enough time to doing it right. But isn't that just another way to justify procrastination? It can be. And when that happens, not only am I upset with myself, the work doesn't get done.

I have learned to counter my inclination to put things off until I can do them perfectly by breaking projects down into smaller steps. I tell myself today I will just do the first step. For instance, if I am working on organizing my kitchen cabinets, I will plan to just gather all the materials the first day. Once that is done, I may feel motivated to go on to the next step. Or not. It's okay. I know I will schedule a time to finish this project at a later date.

Sometimes good enough is good enough.

I use the same trick when I don't feel like exercising. I tell myself I will go to the gym and just do some cardio. Once I am there and get started, I often feel like doing a full workout.

Writing this book has been the same way. Overwhelming is an understatement. I broke it down, starting with an outline. In the beginning, working on one chapter at a time did not sound like a bad idea. However, I found writing the first chapter daunting. I changed gears and started writing notes, and fleshed out the outline until I shifted into writing mode. I started by writing this introduction about me.

Breaking projects down into small steps makes them seem less overwhelming. Scheduling specific times to finish each step is an excellent way to make a big job more manageable.

When I work with a client, I have learned the key is to listen first. I don't make assumptions. I don't jump right in with suggestions or solutions. I apply the skills I honed in my years in the software industry to organizing. First, I gather all the facts. Then I brainstorm with the client. Next we develop a project plan together. Finally, we execute it. A written plan, broken up into categories and steps, is much less overwhelming than no plan at all.

The most important piece of the puzzle is listening. As I work with the client I continue to listen. And if you are organizing your home by yourself, I urge you to keep listening, too.

Do not be so stuck on your original plan you cannot change it. Something may not be working, which means you will have to change course. You may discover doubts or concerns you did not address with the original plan. Adjust along the way.

A key tenet in the software industry is a bug is easier and cheaper to fix in the design phase than it is in the coding phase, or in the testing phase, or once it is released to customers. The same is true with your organization system. The earlier the problem is found and resolved, the better it will be in the long run.

Another benefit of listening first to yourself or your client is you have time to "get it all out." I learned this while working with my software customers. When do you call the software help desk? When you have a problem. If you have a problem, you are not happy. Instead you are frustrated, angry, defensive, argumentative, and rude, or even all of the above.

Allowing someone to vent about the problem diffuses the situation, bringing them back to a normal emotional level so you can calmly discuss the problem. While not exactly the same with my organizing clients, they often feel overwhelmed by the job ahead of them and don't know where to start. Letting clients first talk about it for a while calms them down while building a relationship between us. It builds trust, which is key in organizing.

Becoming a professional organizer was the only path I seriously considered during my transition from employee to business owner. I knew I had the skills, and it would be a job I would love. What could be better? It has been a lot of work becoming my own boss, but it is worth it. I enjoy helping people solve their problems and achieve their goals. I am more than an organizer. I am also a teacher and coach. I help my clients get organized and also show them how to look at their time, their space, and their stuff differently. A change in thinking about what is important, and the real value our stuff has, aids us in getting organized and staying organized so we can better enjoy life.

How to use this book

This book is a guide for clearing the clutter in your home and becoming organized by offering new ways to think about your time, your space, and your stuff, in terms of what is of real value to you. While the book was written to take the reader on a logical journey to organization, chapter by chapter, you may read individual chapters according to your specific interests. Below I provide some suggestions if you plan to skip around.

I share my personal background and path to becoming a professional organizer in the *Introduction*. Definitely read Chapter 1 *Change your thinking* before any subsequent chapters. This chapter provides the foundation for the remaining chapters. Here you will begin to learn new ways to look at your possessions and determine their value as compared to your time and living space.

Chapter 2 *Change your doing* gives some insight as to why we are resistant to change and offers tips on how to overcome this. If you are strongly motivated to make some changes, feel free to skip this chapter.

Chapters 3 and 4 are short chapters on how to *Define the problem* and Make *a plan*, respectively. If you are feeling overwhelmed and do not know where to start, be sure to read these chapters.

If you want to dive right into organizing, jump to Chapter 5 *Start organizing*. Here I provide my basic techniques on how to get organized in a way that will help you stay organized over time.

Chapter 6 *Specific tips* will lead you through the rooms of your home and specific hotspots for clutter and disorganization. Read the chapters that apply to your home and current situation as needed.

Chapter 7 *What comes next?* provides solutions for what to do with all the stuff you have decided to purge from your home, and direction on what to do next now that you have started to get organized.

Lastly, the Appendix provides a list of resources and websites to further help you throughout the organizing process.

Chapter 1
Change your thinking

How did we end up this way? We live in a materialistic, disposable society that values possessions. I have worked with clients in one bedroom apartments and five bedroom homes, and I find they all have the same complaint: There is not enough storage. We fill the space we have, no matter how big or small. In other words, no matter how much space you have to fill, you will fill it. In most cases, though, we are not effectively using our spaces.

We bring things into our homes on a regular basis, but we rarely take the time to look at what we have and remove the unneeded items. We lead busy lives, moving quickly from one activity to the next. We schedule our lives twenty-four hours a day, seven days a week. There is never enough time to do all we want to do, or deal with all we have. We barely have time to relax and enjoy life—so where would we find time to get organized?

To get organized and stay organized, we need to change how we think about our stuff and what is important in our lives, and realize an upfront investment of time and energy will pay off tenfold in the long run.

Why do we stay disorganized?

To be blunt, we stay disorganized because it is easy: easy to do nothing and keep the status quo. By not organizing we don't need to make an effort or make hard decisions. Sometimes we use excuses to justify our decisions to stay disorganized.

"I like my mess." I hear that often from my clients, or from client's spouses who are resistant to change. Fine, you like your mess. But wouldn't you like an organized space better? You know that needed piece of paper is somewhere on your desk, but how much time would you save if the paper was in a specific folder or basket?

"I know where everything is." That is another reason I often hear people give for not getting organized. It may be true. Knowing where it is and finding it quickly and easily can be two different things. Isn't there a better way?

The value of organizing

You may be thinking getting organized will be a lot of work and isn't worth the effort. That depends. It depends on what value you place on saving time and money. Or increasing productivity. Nothing in life is free. Benefits do have a cost. You know you could be better organized, but don't really see the benefit.

Ask yourself these questions:
- Can you park your car in your garage?
- Do you have a cabinet or closet that is so full you cannot really add or remove anything?
- Are you paying for an off-site, external storage unit?

Fill in the blanks:
- I can never find my _____.
- I am always running out of _____.
- I keep buying _____ to find I already had some at home.
- I dread having to do _____ because that space makes me feel anxious, frustrated, or overwhelmed.
- I can always find my _____.
- I never run out of _____.

- I enjoy doing _____.

Getting organized can save you time and money.
- The Small Business Administration estimates eighty percent of filed papers are never looked at again.
- The National Soap and Detergent Association believes getting rid of clutter would eliminate forty percent of the housework in the average home.
- A Harris Interactive study found twenty-three percent of adults say they pay bills late (and incur late fees) because they lose them.
- The Self-Storage Association statistics (there are almost 50,000 self-storage facilities in the US) show that about 9.5 percent of all American households currently rent a self-storage unit, and that has increased from six percent in 1995.[1]

How much time do you waste searching for a specific item? Maybe it's your keys or your glasses. Or a working pen on a desk piled with papers. Or stamps and your checkbook to pay the bills.

Have you ever not paid a bill because you

---

[1] 2015-2016 Self Storage Industry Fact Sheet (as of July 1 2015) Self Storage Association
http://www.selfstorage.org/Library/Public-Library

misplaced it? Did you incur a late fee?

Are your kitchen cabinets packed with cans and jars and bottles and boxes of food?

Do you know what items are in the back of your cabinets or pantry?

How many of the items in your refrigerator have past expiration dates on them?

The National Resource Defense Council estimates American families throw away twenty-five percent of the food and beverages they buy, costing the average family of four anywhere from $1,300 to $2,300 a year.

Think about your current home, and all of your possessions—not only in the living spaces, but everything in the closets, basement, attic, and garage. What if you had to move? Does the thought of packing up all your belongings overwhelm you? What if you needed to sell your home before you can move? Is your home in a condition to show to potential buyers?

> *To get organized and stay organized, we need to change the way we think.*

In business, time is money, and taking too much time can mean lost business. The business lead that is lost in a pile of papers, the customer you forgot to call back, the time-sensitive promotion that expired—little things, such as these, lead to lost business and lost money.

Do you collect something? Artwork, coins, porcelain dolls, vintage beer cans: The variety of items people collect are endless. How is your collection stored and displayed? Is the collection safe and secure? Have items become damaged and as a result lost value? Can you easily enjoy your collection? By organizing your home and your collection you can enjoy what you have and treasure.

What is your favorite room in your home? Why? What is your least favorite? Why? Do your answers have anything to do with the amount of stuff in those rooms? You may love to cook, but if your kitchen is overflowing with pots and pans and gadgets and unopened mail and kid's homework, there probably isn't much room for cooking. How enjoyable can cooking be in such a space? Enjoy the space you have.

One of my clients needed help organizing the workbench in his garage. He is very creative, hard-working, and resourceful, but his workbench was a disaster. Like all of us, he has many responsibilities and not much spare time. While working on projects he did not worry about keeping his workbench neat and tidy. As a result, he suffered from three related symptoms of disorganization: don't know what I have, can't find

Real Value

what I want, and I need it now so let me buy another.

As we sorted his tools together I found four different ratchet sets, three sets of screw drivers, and many open half-full boxes of screws and nails of the same size. The workbench was covered with tools, and hardware and project parts, leaving no room to actually do any work. He would start a new project by moving piles of stuff to one side, clearing just enough space to work.

Organizing his workbench saved him both time and money. He will no longer buy unnecessary duplicate materials. He will not waste time looking for supplies, or clearing his workspace. The upfront investment of a few hours, along with a small amount of regular maintenance, will pay off tenfold as he works on projects in the years to come. It is all about setting up the right systems and developing new habits.

Think about your own home and how organizing specific rooms and clearing clutter would allow you to be more productive. Would an organized kitchen make preparing meals easier? If your desk was clear of paper and supplies, could you be more productive? If the laundry room was neat and orderly, could you do your laundry more efficiently?

John Odalen

Why we hold on to stuff

Very often we are hesitant to get rid of something because we paid good money for it, whether or not we use the item. It's as if keeping the item justifies the purchase or will somehow get our money back. Many years ago, in an attempt to get healthy and lose some weight, I bought a rather expensive elliptical machine. I had the best intentions, and used it for a while, but then it sat there taking up space. I told myself I would start using it again, but I never did. I moved it out of sight to another room in my house. I did not want to sell it as I knew I would not get back what I paid for it. Eventually, I relented and sold it on Craigslist for about half what I paid. Once it was gone I felt a weight lifted, and I had some extra cash. This thinking is quite common and is not unique to expensive items.

> *What is the value of something that you never use?*

A good example of this is a story a friend told me. She was helping her cousin clean out her kitchen when they came across a hot dog cooker in a dusty box. It was obvious the cooker had not been used in years, if ever at all. When my friend suggested to her cousin to discard the cooker, the response was "Oh no, I can't get rid of that, it was

Real Value

a bargain, I got it on sale for five dollars." Not to get too philosophical, but how much is something you never use really worth? My friend's cousin would feel she had wasted that five dollars if she tossed the hot dog cooker. But how much is she wasting by keeping the cooker? How much is that space worth?

Another common justification is the thought we may need it someday. That may be a valid argument, but it's all relative. How much does the item cost? How hard is it to replace? How much space does it take up? How much space do you have? Only you can decide what is more important to helping you achieve your goals: keeping the item or letting it go. If you have the space, it may be easy to keep items you truly do not need. We will talk more about this in Chapter 5.

Some of my clients tell me they want to keep certain items because they like having them. When I hear that, I have to dig deeper. What is the underlying reason for keeping that particular object? What feeling does having the item give the person? How would they feel if they gave up the item?

In many cases, our items hold sentimental value. They bring back memories of good times, or friends and family. We feel giving up the item would mean giving up the memory. Or we feel the person that gifted us the item would be upset if we gave it away. A retired nurse I know wanted to keep all of her old uniforms. They reminded her of work she loved. Did she really need all of them when she never planned to wear them again? Would one or two favorite uniforms serve the same purpose and take up less space?

People hold on to things to make them feel happy. Or successful. Or safe. Someone may be financially stable now, but will hold on to excess just in case the situation changes in the future. "If times get tough, at least I'll have these _____ to use to get by."

All of these reasons speak to how we think about our stuff. If we change our thinking we will have a different perspective and it becomes easier to let go of things we really don't need or no longer want.

The value of stuff

How would you feel if you knew every article of clothing in your closet fit well and was something you loved wearing? Certainly it would take less time getting dressed in the morning.

How do you determine what an item is worth? Is it the amount you paid for it? Or how much you could get if you sold it? That is a common way to value an item, but not the most accurate.

Think about it another way. How much is the item worth to you? What value do you get from it?

Do you use it? Does it bring you joy? Could you live without it?

What value do you get from items you do not use? The expensive kitchen appliance you used once, but now takes up precious cabinet space. The books you read years ago, and enjoyed at the time, but have no plan on rereading. The two dozen handbags and purses crammed in your closet you never use because you favor three other purses. To repurpose a famous saying, "Use it or lose it."

In order to accurately determine the value of something, you need a system to measure it. The easy way is to default to monetary value. Let's start there. Everything has an initial cost—what was paid to acquire the item. Is that the value of the item? Probably not. Unless you are talking about fine jewelry, artwork, or antiques, the current value of the item is less than what was paid for it. If you tried to sell the item today, what could you get for it? You would be lucky to get ten dollars for the old tube television you purchased twenty years ago, considering you can get a new flat screen for a few hundred bucks today.

Instead of getting caught up on how much you paid for something versus what it's worth now, consider how much usage you received from the item. Let's say five years ago you purchased a computer desk for one hundred dollars to put in your home office for your desktop computer. It has served you well. Now you do your work at the dining room table on your laptop. You no longer use the desk, but you paid good money for it, and you also got five years' use from it. That's twenty dollars a year for using the desk. I think you got your money's worth.

We've covered monetary value. But ask yourself, is money the most important thing to you? What about your family? Your health? Your quality of life? Your time? If those things are more important than money, then we should place a higher value on items that contribute to those areas.

Let's consider that computer desk. It has been taking up space for a while now, and has become a clutter magnet. You want to convert your home office to a guest room, but there isn't enough space for a bed, dresser, and the desk in this particular room. When considering the value of the desk, we have to compare it to the value of having a guest room. In this case it is not the monetary value, but the value of your space.

The desk is still in good condition, and you paid good money for it. That can make it harder for you to choose to get rid of it. Maybe you'll put it in the garage with all the other items you no longer use, but cannot part with. Now when considering the value of the desk, we have to compare it to the value of using the garage. If the garage were empty, you could park your car inside in the winter and not have to clear snow off when it storms. How much time would that save you? Is the lost time worth keeping the desk?

When thinking about value, everything is relative. Everything is a choice. Only you can decide what is most important, of the most value. In future chapters we talk about creating a vision for your space and your life, which helps determine value.

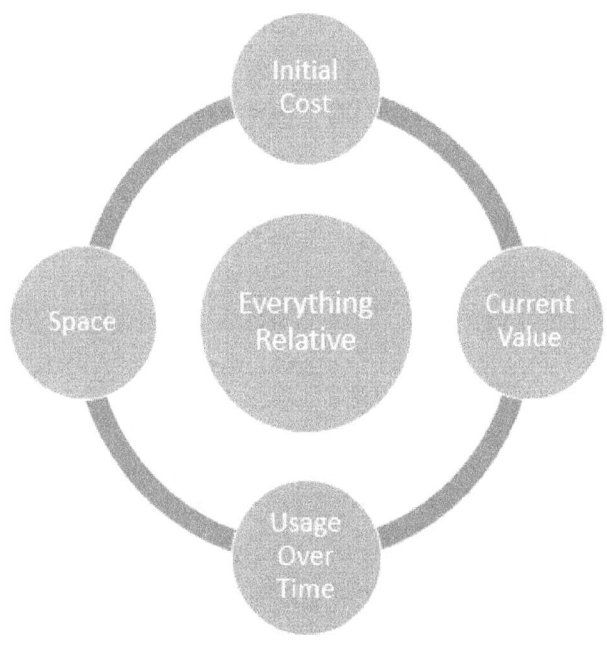

John Odalen

80/20 rule

In science, the Pareto Principle states that eighty percent of results come from twenty percent of causes. This can be applied to many aspects of life. In business it is estimated that eighty percent of sales come from twenty percent of your customers. In software eighty percent of the defects are found in only about twenty percent of the code.

When it comes to our stuff quite often eighty percent of the time we are only using twenty percent of our possessions. The rest just sits idle, maybe to be used in the future, but probably not. Think about your wardrobe. Do you wear the same clothes week in and week out? How many shirts are in your closet but are never worn, either because they don't fit, don't look good on you, have gone out of style, or you just don't like them? Are you still keeping that 1970's leisure suit? The 1980's leg warmers? The wide legged pants from the 1990's? The T-shirts from the 10K you ran in 2010?

Physical clutter leads to mental clutter

As I mentioned earlier in the book, some people can work amidst the clutter. But others cannot. Clutter can be a distraction, whether consciously or subconsciously. Consciously you may think about the clutter and not the important task at hand. Or subconsciously you may feel uncomfortable or unable to work well in certain spaces because they are cluttered, even if you don't consciously realize the reason.

A few times while writing this book I had to stop and completely clean my desk before I could begin writing. I couldn't focus. It wasn't only the physical clutter distracting me, but the nagging sense something in the pile of papers needed attention and was more important than writing.

We all lead busy lives with family obligations, work responsibilities, and social engagements. Our brains get filled with to-do lists, thoughts about what we are doing right now and what needs to be done later. We worry something won't get done. Our physical clutter adds to those feelings of chaos. We become overloaded and cannot focus on any one thing.

And then what?

We all have good intentions when it comes to our stuff. When considering whether or not to keep something, ask yourself "And then what?" What is the plan for keeping this item?

Consider this. You recently lost some weight, and now have clothes in two different sizes. You are hesitant to discard the larger size clothes, so you pack them away. And then what? What is the plan for these clothes? Keep them forever in the event you gain the weight back? By keeping the larger size clothes are you giving yourself permission to gain the weight back? Or setting the expectation that you will gain it back?

Asking "and then what?" is especially helpful when dealing with sentimental items. Take your children's artwork for an example. In the early years kids create volumes of art. Some good, some mediocre, some downright awful. Do you need to keep every drawing? The answer depends upon many factors, including how much space you are willing to dedicate to storing it all.

If you had unlimited space, would you save everything? What would be the end result? What is the plan? To store forever, never to be looked at again? To bring out on holidays to show the relatives? To hand off the boxes of art to your children when they are grown? Will your children want it? Knowing the end game makes deciding what to keep much easier. We'll talk more on solutions in Chapter 6.

Chapter 2
Change your doing

Change is not easy, but it is also not impossible. If change was easy, there wouldn't be thousands of self-help books on all different subjects. We are creatures of habit; we are comfortable with the familiar and prefer things to stay the same.

Change can be emotional. For some people, change can be overwhelming, or scary, or even panic inducing, and any change should be made very gradually. Too severe a change in a short period of time may have disastrous side effects and disrupt the process of making the change and make it even more difficult for the person to accept.

Change takes time. It takes time to work on the

new behavior or physical activity. It also takes time to implement the change and convert it from something that feels new and uncomfortable into a regular, daily behavior.

Getting organized involves taking the time and making the effort to process all of your stuff. It may require some physical changes to your environment. But that is only half the battle. Staying organized requires developing and practicing new habits so you can maintain what you have achieved so far.

How long does it take to form a new habit? In the 1960s, Maxwell Maltz theorized in his book *Psycho-Cybernetics* it takes a minimum of twenty-one days to adjust to and accept change. Since then countless writers, coaches, motivational speakers, and self-help gurus have taken that belief, stated it as fact, and run with it. Some have said, "In just twenty-one days you can…," while others have even offered a whole new way of life in just one month, and so on. But what is the truth?

Recently Phillippa Lally[2] published a study in the *European Journal of Social Psychology* that concluded everyone is different and will take a different length of time to develop a new habit.

---

[2] Phillippa Lally*, Cornelia H. M. van Jaarsveld, Henry W. W. Potts and Jane Wardle. How are habits formed: Modelling habit formation in the real world. Article first published online: 16 JUL 2009 DOI: 10.1002/ejsp.674

Participants' timeframes ranged from 18 to 254 days. But on average, it takes 66 days for the new habit to become routine.

I tend to be on the shorter end of the range when implementing a new behavior. After a few weeks my new routine becomes a habit. Then again I like structure. That means it is also easy for me to "fall off the wagon." If I stray from my routine for a few days it is so easy for me to give it up and get off track.

For example, I enjoy going to the gym first thing in the morning. I like the sense of accomplishment I feel when I start my day having accomplished something. It also gives me extra energy. However, if I stop going for a few days, no matter how valid the reasons, it becomes difficult for me to get back on track. I need to use my mental tricks to motivate myself back to the gym a few days in a row. The longer I've been away, the longer it takes to regain the momentum.

Like most people, if I'm not invested in making a change, it won't happen. I've tried many times to keep a food journal. I've been told keeping track of the food you eat is an excellent tool for eating a healthier diet and losing weight. Periodically I resolve to keep track of everything I eat. For the first week or so I start out enthusiastically writing down every morsel of food I put in my mouth, but then I begin to lose interest and start making excuses. I'm late for a meeting, so I don't get my breakfast entries made. The next day I eat dinner at a restaurant, and don't track the food. Pretty soon I quit tracking what I eat altogether. I never cross over from starting a new routine to making the tracking of my food a habit. I haven't given up though. I'll keep trying.

Is it difficult for you to transfer from getting organized to staying organized—all the time? How do you overcome your natural resistance to change? Consider the Formula for Change, developed by David Gleicher in the early 1960's[3] and updated by Kathie Dannemiller in the 1980's.[4]

Formula for Change

$D \times V \times F > R$

D = Dissatisfaction with how things are now
V = Vision for the future
F = First steps to take
R = Resistance

The product of the three factors needed for change must be greater than the resistance. In other

---

[3] Cady, S.H., Jacobs, J., Koller, R., & Spalding, J. (2014). The change formula: Myth, legend, or lore. OD Practitioner, 46(3), 32–39.

[4] Wheatley, M. J., Tannebaum, R., Yardley, P. Y., & Quade, K. (2003). Organization development at work: Conversations on the values, applications, and future of OD (pp. 62–64). San Francisco, CA: John Wiley & Sons.

Real Value

words, you have to want the change and be willing to take action more than anything getting in your way. If you have no dissatisfaction with the way things are now, then there is no desire to change.

The same is true if you have no vision for the future. If you are not working toward something better, there will be no change. Lastly, if you take no action, no change will occur. If any one of these elements is missing, resistance always win. You don't actually enter numbers for each variable, but instead a relative value.

Let's use a common goal as an example: losing weight. There are several familiar reasons, or **dissatisfactions,** why you want to lose weight. You may be dissatisfied with your appearance, with the actual number you see when you step on the scale, with how your clothes fit, your physical fitness, a specific weight-relation medical problem, or any combination of the above.

Your **vision for the future**, or goal, may be to reach a specific weight goal, or clothing size, or it may just be an image of how you will look at a lesser weight.

Weight loss typically involves changing diet and exercising, so your **first steps** might be to see a doctor or a nutritionist, read a healthy eating book, or take a daily walk.

Applying the formula, the level of dissatisfaction with the current state times the level of desire and commitment to achieve the vision times the level of effort needed to make the first steps must be greater than the **resistance to change**. If any of these factors are missing (in other words, are a zero), resistance will always be higher. However, if your dissatisfaction and desire are high, even if your effort is low, the product may still be greater than the resistance, and change will occur. Change may happen slowly, but it will happen.

What is resistance?

How do we define resistance? Resistance is anything that gets in the way and prevents the change. Resistance comes in many forms. It may be the extra time and effort you need to take the first steps. For example, you decide to go back to school to pursue a better career. That may mean working days, school at nights, homework on weekends, leaving little time for social activities. In other words, having to give up something in the short term in order to reach your long term goal.

In the example of weight loss, changing your diet and giving up some of your favorite less healthy foods will be hard. Resistance can also be a mental roadblock, such as telling yourself you won't succeed, or aren't good enough, or the pain isn't really worth the reward. For each of us resistance is different. The challenge is to ensure the other side of the equation is much stronger than the resistance.

Let's look at this in terms of getting organized. Say your garage is packed so full of stuff you cannot park your car inside. You have so much stuff just thrown about you can never find what you are looking for. Some boxes have fallen over. Some holiday decorations are damaged. However much this troubles you would be your level of dissatisfaction.

Now for the flip side: What is your vision for the future? It might be a spacious garage, with only the needed items inside, organized nicely on shelves on the sides and back of the garage leaving enough room to park your car inside. Perfect. Now what are your first steps? Maybe scheduling an afternoon with the family to clean out the garage so you can decide what should be kept and what can be sold or tossed. This is just a first step. Maybe after the initial sort and purge, you'll need to buy some shelving.

Now let's look at the resistance. In this case, resistance means time and energy. It will take at least a few hours for the initial sorting and purging session. You want the entire family to be involved, so you need to coordinate schedules. There certainly may be some resistance from family members. There may be some heavy lifting and moving of items, so you all need to be well rested.

Which side of the equation is greater? Your desire for the neat and organized garage, or all of the steps needed to get the garage that way?

As you can see, getting organized takes time, effort, and a change in your thinking. In the next three chapters I will help you clarify your personal dissatisfaction with your organization, develop a vision of how you would like your space to look, and identify the necessary first steps you need to take to get and stay organized.

Chapter 3
Define the problem

It's become almost a cliché to say "the first step to fixing a problem is admitting you have one." As with most clichés, there is a lot of truth in that statement. The first step to getting organizing is identifying there is a need for improvement in some part of your home or life.

Once you admit there is a problem, your second step is to begin to figure out exactly what those problem areas are. Is your messy kitchen driving you crazy? Can you never find the clothing you're looking for because your bedroom closet is disorganized? Would you love to park your car inside your garage, but it won't fit because of all the boxes stored there?

Do not worry about possible solutions at this point. Just think about the problems. What really frustrates you? What would you like to improve?

Get a journal for keeping your plans for getting organized and start making notes in it. Keep the journal with you throughout the day. Thoughts may pop into your head at any time. When they do, stop and write them down. During your day you will probably experience problems in one or more of the areas you identified. Make notes as you experience the problems. If you wait until later, you will forget.

Continue to make notes. This process should take a few days. There is no rush. You didn't become overwhelmed by too much stuff in one day; it will take more than one day to solve the problem.

Clutter happens

Clutter happens when items don't have a permanent home convenient to where the item is used. Think about what ends up on your kitchen counter or island: mail, newspapers, keys, purse, homework, receipts etc.. Do they belong here? Do they have another home? Should they have another home?

Most flat surfaces are clutter magnets. Sometimes I struggle to keep my desktop clear. It is too easy to put something down and move on to the next paper or task. In Chapter 6, I will share how I keep this from becoming out of control.

Clutter also happens when we don't have a routine to combat clutter and allow ourselves to follow bad habits. How much more effort would it take to hang up a coat instead of tossing it on the back of the sofa?

Too much stuff

Doing laundry is a fact of life. It is never ending. After you wash, dry, and fold your clothes, do you put them in your closet or dresser? Or do you live out of your laundry basket? If the latter, is the reason because you are lazy (probably not) or because your closets and dressers are so packed that it is difficult or impossible to put items away properly?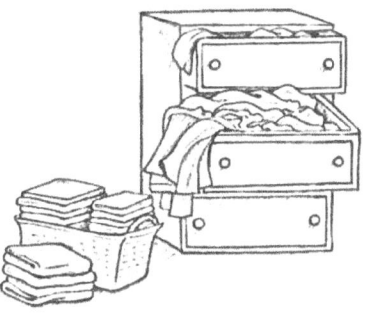

When you think of clutter, you may immediately think of someone with too much stuff. Or not enough storage. Or both. Since storage space is finite, downsizing your possessions is usually one step in getting organized. Using what was discussed in Chapter 1 concerning real value, and the tips we will cover in Chapter 5, you will be able to make decisions on what items you need and what you should keep.

Identify what is not working

Think about your home and your stuff. What frustrates you? What daily tasks do you dread because of the disorganization and/or overload of stuff?

- Grooming
- Dressing
- Preparing meals
- Eating
- Homework
- Paying bills
- Home-based business
- Laundry and ironing
- Housecleaning
- Yardwork
- Household chores

Now is the time to dream and build your vision. Don't worry about the how. Pretend you can snap your fingers and immediately make a change. What would you change?

Now keep things within reason—you are bound by reality—but write down your true wish list. Your list may be long, but don't feel overwhelmed by the work ahead. Think about the opportunities for making your life easier. Anything is possible. In the next chapter, I will discuss how to make a plan that is specific, measurable, and achievable.

Chapter 4
Make a plan

Create a vision

A key factor in achieving any goal is having a vision to work toward. In the case of organizing the vision will have a few parts. First, you want to think about how your life will improve by getting organized. Will you be able to prepare and eat meals in a clutter-free kitchen, or what you will do in your free time once you are organized?

Second, visualize the physical space. Imagine each room clutter-free, everything in its place. What does it look like to you?

Lastly, think about how you want the space to make you feel. Currently, you may feel overwhelmed or anxious, unproductive, angry, frustrated, tired. Your new space should make you feel calm, relaxed, creative, productive, peaceful, welcoming.

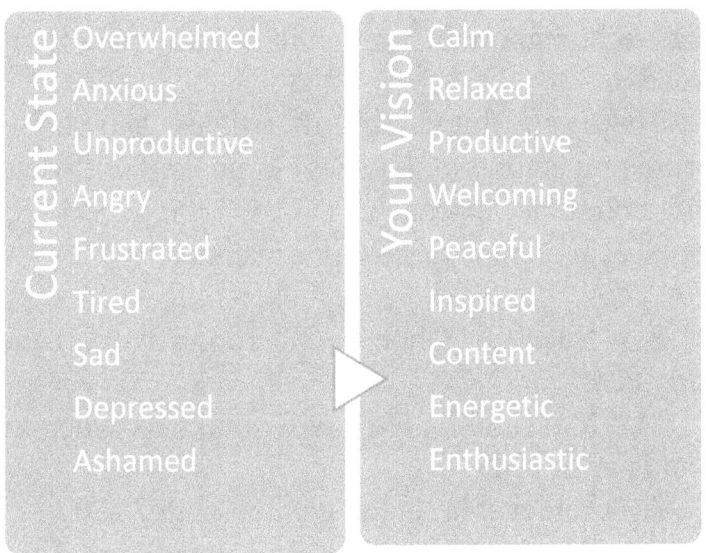

Current State	Your Vision
Overwhelmed	Calm
Anxious	Relaxed
Unproductive	Productive
Angry	Welcoming
Frustrated	Peaceful
Tired	Inspired
Sad	Content
Depressed	Energetic
Ashamed	Enthusiastic

Collecting pictures from magazines or on the internet can be helpful in creating and focusing on your vision. Use anything that keeps you motivated. One bit of advice on this—do not get caught up in achieving perfection. I will talk more about this in Chapter 5; perfection is not required to get organized. Pictures in magazines can be unrealistic or impractical, showing living spaces where no one lives. If picture perfect is your vision, then go for it. But just know that good enough is good enough.

Set goals

To get organized and stay organized you need to set goals. Have a purpose. Work toward something. Your goals need to be more important to you than keeping unneeded items. Your goals need to be important enough to allocate time to the process.

There are hundreds of articles and books written on setting and achieving goals. I will share one common approach, called setting SMART goals, as it applies to getting organized.

S – Specific: Choose one room, work zone, daily task

M – Measurable: How will you know when the goal is achieved?

A – Achievable: Is the goal possible?

R – Results Focused: Why are you doing this goal?

T – Time Bound: What is your deadline?

Here is an example: This weekend, I want to clean out and organize my food pantry so I can see all the contents, and easily create a shopping list so I buy only what I need, and so I use food before it expires.

Each of these elements is vital in defining a goal. Writing down your goal will increase your chances of accomplishing it.

Prioritize

Look at your vision and your goals. What is most important to you? Which areas give you the most grief? When organized, which areas would save you the most time or money or energy?

Let's say you created your vision for a clutter-free home and set your goals to organize your bedroom closet, the kitchen cabinets, counters, and table, your home office, and the garage.

Downsizing your wardrobe and organizing the bedroom closet will allow you to get dressed faster before work and let you wear new clothes you bought months ago, but are still in the bags. Organizing the kitchen will make meal prep much easier for you and also create a clean, welcoming space for eating meals and doing homework for the entire family. Organizing your home office will make monthly bill paying less of a chore. Cleaning out the garage will allow you to park your car in the garage instead of in the driveway.

Which is your top priority? There is no right or wrong answer. Only you can decide. If you are often late to work, maybe your bedroom closet comes first. Or since you and the family spend the most time in the kitchen, that is your top priority. Or maybe winter is coming and you really want to park your car in the garage so you don't have to clear off the snow in the morning. Trust your instincts and pick one area. The others will follow shortly.

Chapter 5
Start organizing

You have defined your problem areas and set your goals. You have your vision. Now you are ready to start organizing. The project may still feel overwhelming. Where do you start?

There is no one right way to begin to organize your space. In this chapter I will give you suggestions to help you to think about your project, a plan for how to get started on it, and some basic steps for getting organized.

Start small

Getting organized doesn't have to be an all or nothing proposal. It's actually easier if done in small steps.

Begin with one room, or a closet, or even a drawer. Tell yourself you will organize for ten minutes and then move on. I recently went to my best friend's house for dinner. After dinner, while she was putting her son to bed, I decided to unload the dishwasher for her. I noticed the cabinet with her storage containers looked like a messy toy box, with containers and lids and some other miscellaneous kitchen items put wherever there was space. I took everything out and sorted the containers into shapes and sizes, matching containers with lids, and separating the smaller ones used for her son's lunches. Within ten minutes I had everything back in the cabinet in logical groups, along with a few orphan containers and lids I suggested my friend toss. I'm not suggesting you do anything like this without asking first—I knew my friend wouldn't mind. My point is organizing doesn't have to be a large time-consuming project.

Apply this technique to your home. Determine what area bothers you the most. If you can't tackle it in a short amount of time, break it into smaller chunks. If your clothes closet frustrates you, start with your pants one day. The next day look at your dresses. Whenever you have more time tackle your shoes. Eventually the entire closet will be organized.

Work zones

A key strategy for getting organized and staying organized is to create work zones. They can be entire rooms, a section of a room, or even one drawer or shelf. A work zone can be thought of as an area where you do a specific task and everything you need for that task is readily available in the zone. Or determine what is the function of this area, and anything that is not needed for that function does not belong here.

A kitchen is a work zone. In the kitchen you cook and eat. Your food, dishes, cookware, plates, and utensils are all stored in the kitchen. What if we break it down further? You may have a coffee zone with the coffee maker, coffee, filters, mugs, spoons, and sugar all within the same section of the kitchen. Ideally this would be near the refrigerator for easy access to the milk or cream, but we are bound by physical limitations. It doesn't have to be perfect.

Many people have a home office zone in the kitchen. Keeping the home office supplies separate from the regular kitchen supplies helps you stay organized. What if the home office zone is the kitchen table? Instead of a permanent work zone, use baskets for work supplies that can be moved out of the way during meals.

Real Value

Work zones do not need to be connected with an activity, but instead are connected with a purpose. Storage areas are one example. A closet may be dedicated to jackets and coats only, or to long-term storage of holiday decorations. When every space has a purpose, and only items germane to that purpose live there, you have a better chance of staying organized.

My family likes to entertain. For over thirty years every summer my parents host a barbeque for about a hundred people. You would think they would need to rent supplies to host so many people. They don't. Over the years, they have acquired all they need, but you wouldn't know by it looking at their home during the year.

My mother keeps all her entertaining supplies neatly organized. For many years they were stored in several different locations around the house. There were extra folding chairs in the basement, paper plates and plastic utensils in the kitchen, the paper decorations in the hall closet. She always knew where everything was stored, but the rest of the family only had a general

> How much time would you save if, when you needed something, you knew exactly where to find it.

idea. If they needed supplies during the rest of the year, they always had to ask her where specific items, such as the extra paper cups, were located.

At the back of their house are two coat closets. A few years ago I convinced my mother to consolidate and purge some of the coats to free up one closet for all her party supplies. I removed the single rod and installed shelving, floor to ceiling. Together we gathered all her supplies in the dining room and did a quick sort and purge. Everything left was organized neatly in the new closet space. Now she has year-round easy access to everything.

The moderate sized shed in the backyard is packed with tables and chairs, tents, coolers, grills, and other larger party supplies, in addition to the regular outdoor stuff such as the lawn mower and snow blower. It all fits because everything has its place, and every spot is utilized. This is my father's domain. Every year after the party, instead of loading the shed haphazardly, he carefully puts everything back in its place, making adjustments as needed. When the next year rolls around, setting up for the barbeque is easy because everything needed is accessible.

Benefits of work zones

There are many good reasons to organize your home into work zones. Here are a few:

1. You will always know where to find the item.

   Think of how much time and energy you would save if, when you needed something, you knew exactly where to find it. Whether it is your car keys, or extra pens, or a flashlight, you can count on it always being in the same spot. This is even more helpful with less frequently used items. The gravy boat that is only used on holidays, or the shoe shine kit you haven't used in a few years but you have a formal event coming up and need it.

2. You won't be looking through unrelated items.

   Everyone has a kitchen junk drawer, with little things that don't seem to have a home. Do you also have a cabinet or closet that holds a little bit of everything? The place you shove stuff when company is coming over? Now imagine you need something that you think is in that space. Does the expression "needle in a haystack" come to mind? By creating work zones, we eliminate these black holes of storage.

3. Items are located convenient to the task.

   You need to pay some bills. You keep the bills in the kitchen, but where is your checkbook? In your home office, or your purse. Where are the stamps? In a cup in the dining room china cabinet. You also need a pen. Wouldn't it be easier if everything was in a single drawer or basket or bin?

John Odalen

Perfection not required

Just as we are all unique individuals, we all have different ways of processing information, different habits, learning styles, aesthetics, etc. We also have different ways of getting and staying organized. It's important that the system works for you and that it can be maintained.

Let's consider paperwork. You may want a detailed file system with folders for every possible category and subcategory, in color coded and alphabetized files. Or you may be satisfied with only a few files to cover the large topics, such as home, finance, medical, etc. Or some level of detail in between those two. Whatever system works for you that allows you to find what you need when you need it, and can be maintained, is the right way for *you* to organize.

Getting organized does not need to cost anything. You don't need to spend lots of money on storage solutions. You can start by using everyday household items to try out the new system. A big mistake people make when trying to get organized is to start with lots of baskets and bins or complicated and expensive organizational systems. Buying storage solutions should be your last step. Once you determine exactly what needs to be organized you may find that you don't need anything new. It is also a good idea to try out the system first before spending money. You can use empty shoe boxes to test a system, and if it works, replace the shoe boxes with decorative baskets.

Speaking of storage solutions, remember your space doesn't need to look like a picture in a magazine. It doesn't have to be pretty. Shoe boxes may be acceptable to you. If they are in a closet and not on display, who cares if they aren't a beautifully patterned and matching basket set?

Sort, review, purge, organize

A key step to getting organized is to look at all of your stuff and decide what to keep and what to toss. In order to do that effectively, though, you need to have everything together that fits in one category.

For example, if you have some books in the bedroom, others in the family room, and more in the home office, bring them together in one place so you can see your total collection. This is only an interim step. When you are done sorting and reviewing, you will return your books to where they came from, or you might decide on a better organizational system. More on that later.

Next decide what is an appropriate number of books to keep. Then start reviewing. As you review, you may need to sort further in order to help you make decisions. Fiction in one pile, nonfiction in another, reference in a third. Do

John Odalen

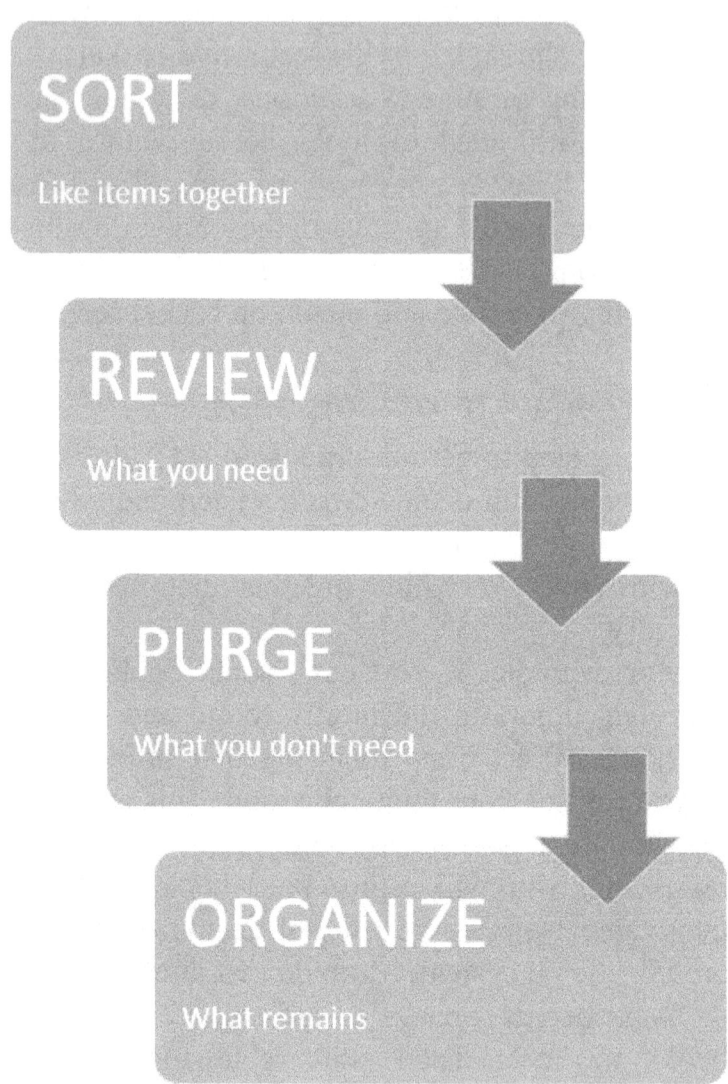

whatever you need to do to understand what you have.

When reviewing and purging, it is important to define your criteria for what to keep before you begin the process. Then stick to that criteria.

Here are some suggestions for developing your criteria.

What will fit in existing space?

For example, suppose you have a shoe rack that fits twelve pairs of shoes. But you have twenty-four pairs of shoes. You can decide up front you will only keep twelve pairs to fit inside the rack. The rest have to go. Or decide to store the out of season shoes elsewhere. Keep in mind that by keeping more shoes, you may need to give up something else down the line. If you are a book lover, you may decide only to keep books that will fit in a bookcase, and donate the rest to the library. If you collect ceramic birds, you may decide only to keep as many as fit comfortably in a curio cabinet. You get the idea.

How many do you really need?

For your wardrobe, decide how many shirts, skirts, pants, sweaters, etc., is practical and reasonable for one person to have, taking into consideration what you actually wear. For example, maybe you have certain outfits you only wear to the office. How many different outfits do you need? What is practical? Two weeks' worth? Three? Can you mix and match to create new looks? Or maybe you have a dozen sweaters but you really aren't a sweater person. You may only wear a sweater when it is extremely cold. How many sweaters do you need?

Love it, need it, or use It?

When deciding what items you will keep, ask yourself the following three questions: Do you love it? Do you need it? Do you use it? If you cannot answer yes to at least one of those questions, you should discard the item.

Let's break it down.

Do you love it? Does the item make you feel good? Do you like looking at the item or having it around? Does it enhance your life? Consider your wardrobe. Why keep an article of clothing that doesn't look all that great on you, or you don't feel great wearing, or you never ever wear?

Do you use it? Is the item used regularly? A good example is the vacuum. Used on a regular basis. You need to keep it. But what about a carpet steam cleaner. You received it as a gift, but have never used it. You only have a few carpets in your home. You are limited on space. Consider selling or donating it. If you need to clean a carpet, you can rent a unit or hire a professional.

Do you need it? Some items are rarely used, but still need to be kept. A fire extinguisher. Your birth certificate. A first aid kit.

Keep in mind these are guidelines when sorting and purging. Decisions must still be based in reality. You may not love your sofa, but unless you can afford to replace it, it does not make sense to discard it.

I recently had to treat myself as a client to deal with a situation in my kitchen: I bought a new microwave. I had wanted a new one for a few years. My old one still works, but it was small and not powerful enough. After saving some gift cards and doing the research, I finally decided it was time. I love the new microwave, but it is bigger than the old one. My old microwave lived inside a large cabinet next to the stove. I loved being able to shut the door and hide the microwave. The cabinet is large enough to provide some extra storage for cutting boards and sheet pans. Now there is no room for that. I was forced to make some changes.

When it comes to kitchen tools and gadgets, I have a hard time purging. I know it must be done from time to time. In this case I could have shoved the excess gadgets to another cabinet and lived with it. I knew, though, very soon I would become frustrated by the overflow. I also could have moved some things around and stored some of the items in the oven, like many people do. Again, not for me.

What did I do instead? I took all the baking equipment out from one smaller cabinet and the storage drawer under the oven. Seeing everything together, I decided what I really needed and used and what I could do without. Then I packed up what was unneeded and put it in my car with the old microwave to donate to charity. I didn't ponder each item. I trusted my gut and went with the facts of how often or when I last used each item. The process only took me about half an hour. It was well worth it.

Does it fit?

This is an easy question to apply to clothing. If it doesn't fit right now, why are you keeping it? I have many clients who fluctuate between sizes so they keep two or three different wardrobes. All in one closet. Unless the closet is huge, I suggest packing away clothes that are too small or too big until you need them.

Styles change. If you are keeping clothes from five years ago hoping they will fit someday, when that day comes, will you actually want to wear them? Or will you want to buy new clothes to show off your new figure? On the flip side, are you keeping large size clothes just in case you gain weight? By doing so, are you telling yourself you will eventually regain the weight?

Does it fit into your life right now? We all have different hobbies; some come and go, and some stay throughout our lifetime. If you have a hobby that lives only in the past, it is time to part with all the associated equipment and accessories, so you can focus on the present.

Is it damaged or broken?

We live in a disposable society. Items are cheap to buy, cheap to replace, and are not made to last very long.

Something breaks and we think "I'll fix that" or "it's still good." And the item ends up sitting and taking up space. Either set a deadline for getting it fixed, or toss it. Don't let it live in limbo.

With clothing, anything ripped or stained that cannot be repaired or cleaned should be discarded. No discussion. You say it's good to wear for painting or cleaning or as my mother says "knocking around the house"? Fine. How many of those outfits do you have? How many do you need? Be honest with yourself.

Maximize your space

Would you like a bigger home? I bet all of us would. But would that solve any problems? I have worked with clients in varying size homes, from small apartments to modest houses to large mansions. Almost always every closet and drawer, every inch of the basement or garage, has been filled and still my client has clutter. The answer is not more space. We tend to fill the space we have. One part of the solution is to maximize the space you have, using it to the fullest potential.

This may mean taking advantage of hidden storage, such as benches or chests that also double as seating. Or going vertical with shelving or cabinets, or hanging items from a garage ceiling.

> *The answer is not more space!*

You can also maximize your space by looking for the best storage solutions for a space, and the right items to be stored in certain spaces.

Let's consider the traditional clothes closet with one shelf and one hanging rod. The shelf is sometimes too high to pile clothes without the entire pile falling when you try to get something from it—particularly if the "something" is on the bottom of the pile. You might use small baskets to keep like clothes together. Or use this space for less frequently used items or off-season clothing. The space under the hanging rod and clothes typically becomes a catchall for shoes, luggage, unused items, or things that fall from the shelf. A freestanding shelving unit or large basket will help keep things in place.

Using some of the previous tactics, including downsizing possessions, and creating work zones will help you maximize your space. Keep only what you need where you need it. Less frequently used items can be stored in the basement, attic, or garage and retrieved when needed.

Labeling

Labeling is a great tool to help you stay organized. You can easily find where something is when you need it, or where something goes when you need to put it away.

I have been a fan of Julia Child since I was a child watching her shows on PBS. I was too young to cook, but I still watched. What does that have to do with getting organized? I loved her kitchen. Her husband, Paul, famously organized her home kitchen by hanging her pots and pans and utensils on the pegboard wall (great use of vertical storage, maximizing your space) and tracing the outline of each item so Julia knew where everything belonged. I'm not suggesting you draw on your walls, but some labeling and creativity can go a long way.

Label shelves in cabinets or a pantry. Label storage boxes with the contents for easy retrieval. Label electronics wires. A few minutes spent up front will be saved time and again down the road.

Supplies for organizing

Before you begin organizing, you may be tempted to purchase new bins and baskets and trays. Please don't. First, you cannot evaluate what organizational solutions you may need until you have sorted and reviewed and purged what you have. Second, you may already have items in your home that will work.

While you do not need anything to start organizing, having these few supplies handy will help:

>Notepad and pen for notes
>Markers
>Masking tape or white labels
>Garbage bag for trash and recycle
>Bags or boxes for sell or donate
>One box for items that belong elsewhere

As discussed earlier in this chapter, you will be sorting your items, and then reviewing to decide what to keep and what to purge. As you make decisions, it will be helpful to separate these items into the broad categories (rehome, sell, donate, recycle, toss) and package them up for the next step. Have the necessary supplies on hand while you work. Label the boxes and bags and put them aside until the charity truck comes or you are ready for your yard sale. You might want to designate one area of the home as a staging area for anything already decided on. Otherwise, you may be tempted to sift through the next day and second-guess your decisions.

While you are organizing a given space, you will come across items that do not belong in that space. Instead of stopping what you are doing to put the item back where it belongs, allocate one box as a "lost and found" for items that go elsewhere. When you have finished your organizing session, you can deal with the items in the box.

Chapter 6
Specific tips

In this chapter, we will cover popular areas of the home and categories of items that lead to clutter, discuss different ways to look at these spaces and the value of these items, and how to organize them effectively. The general strategies covered in Chapter 5 will still apply—work zones, 80/20 rule, criteria for keeping items, maximize your space—but additional detailed strategies will be discussed for each area.

Clothes

Most of us have too much stuff of one kind or another, but the one category I can usually count on my customers having too much of is clothing. We all have too many clothes. We fill our closets and drawers and still keep buying more. Rarely do we purge anything. Whether or not we spent a lot of money on a piece of clothing, whether or not we wear it, we have a hard time letting go.

The general tips I covered in Chapter 5 apply to our wardrobes. When organizing your clothes, the key is to be realistic and honest with yourself and to set limits. Here is a list of some questions to ask yourself as you go through your clothing, and that of other family members.

- Does it fit?
- Is it ripped or stained?
- Is it in style?
- Do I like wearing it?
- Does it look good on me?
- When was the last time I wore it?
- How many X do I really need?
- How much space do I have?

The easiest way to proceed is to work on just one part of your wardrobe at a time, for instance, look only at your sweaters in one session, only at shoes in the next, and so on. Make sure to review everything you have that fits into that category, and keep in mind you will probably be buying new clothes in the future. If you don't leave enough space for new purchase, one more pair of jeans or a new dress might put you instantly back on the road to disorganization, If you only have enough space on your shelf for five sweaters and you know you will purchase three more in the year, where will you put them? Now is the time to decide.

Kitchen and pantry

Of all the rooms in the house, I feel that work zones are most beneficial in the kitchen. You have a mix of hard goods (dinnerware, flatware, pots and pans, glasses, mugs, appliances, etc.) and soft goods (refrigerated foods, canned and boxed goods, spices, etc.). Also many different tasks and activities are done in the kitchen. You prepare meals here, but that is too broad a category to consider when organizing. Making coffee, preparing breakfast, packing lunches, cooking dinner, holiday baking: All of these tasks have different needs. Think about where in the kitchen you do each task, what you need to do it, and where those items are currently stored. Is this the best location? Is there a better one?

Once you decide what goes where, you can move on to deciding what is needed. Use the techniques discussed in Chapter 5 to help you determine what you should keep and what should be tossed. How many odd coffee mugs do you need? Which kitchen gadgets are never used? How many different sized baking dishes are appropriate? When making decisions, think about your day-to-day use of the kitchen, as well as how you use it on special occasions, how much space you actually have, and your vision for the space.

Earlier, I talked about Julia Child's kitchen. My mother could never live with Julia's kitchen.

She likes everything put away, out of sight, and her kitchen looking spotless. For me function is more important. I have utensils and measuring cups hanging on the wall next to my stove, right where I need them. I had a dedicated knife drawer, but would rather keep my knives on the counter where I can reach them with ease.

When it comes to food storage, in addition to organizing for the different tasks and available space, we also must consider food waste and overbuying. The classic example of this is buying another jar of nutmeg at Thanksgiving because you cannot find the one you bought last year, only to find that old jar once you start baking. Are your kitchen cabinets and pantry so jammed packed that you cannot see what is in the back? Do you have any packaged food that has expired? After you sort, review, and purge, decide what a practical limit is for each type of food item. Organize like items together so you can see exactly what you have.

Are the cabinets above the refrigerator hardly used? Take a picture of the contents and post the picture on the inside of another cabinet door with similar items for an easy reminder of what is there. This tip can also be used for any other remote storage areas.

How else do you use your kitchen?

The kitchen has become the hub of the home. It is often used for more than preparing and eating meals. If other items are to be stored in the kitchen for other tasks, try to create separate work zones to keep things orderly. Whether it is art supplies for the kids, or paperwork for the adults, dedicating a small space for the task and supplies will help keep the entire room clutter-free. Baskets and bins are another option for work that gets done in the kitchen or dining room. Related supplies can be stored in the basket and taken out when needed. When not in use, the baskets can be stored off to the side or, when company comes over, in another room entirely. Think portable work zone.

Toiletries, medicines, and makeup

Personal care products are another big category for my clients. We all have an arsenal of products we use on a daily basis that need to be replenished. To save time and money, we buy in bulk. And sometimes we keep buying, more than we could practically use. We buy products for a specific circumstance, use a bit, and leave the product on the shelf. We try a new product, use a bit, decide we don't care for it, and leave the product on the shelf.

Personal care products should be reviewed at least twice a year, ideally once every three months. If done frequently, the process should only take a few minutes and the effort will be worth it. Keep only what you use, need, or love.

Items with expiration dates, such as medicine, makeup, and some toiletries, require no thinking. If the item is expired, toss it. Certain medicines can be disposed by flushing. See Appendix for more info.

Makeup is very personal. Either you like it or you don't; either it looks good on you or it doesn't. If you don't like it, get rid of it. Don't put it back in the drawer hoping maybe you will use it someday. You won't. If it can be used by someone else, such as a friend or family member, give it away or else toss it in the trash. Keeping it won't bring your money back.

Paperwork and home office

As much as we try to "go paperless," there will always be paperwork coming into the home. It is unavoidable but not unmanageable. Here are some tips to help organize your paperwork.

- Eliminate as much incoming paper as possible and practical.
- Use a basket for all incoming mail and paperwork that needs to be reviewed and processed.
- Process this basket on a set schedule (daily or weekly).

- Immediately discard and/or shred any junk mail, outer envelopes, and extraneous flyers.
- Move only the important papers to the next stage of an action folder or file drawer.

There are many ways to organize paperwork. You may need to try a few systems before you settle on one that works well for you. Some people want every piece of paper filed away, while others like to create piles, having everything within reach at all times. As a compromise, I prefer using baskets to keep like papers together. For example, I have one basket for 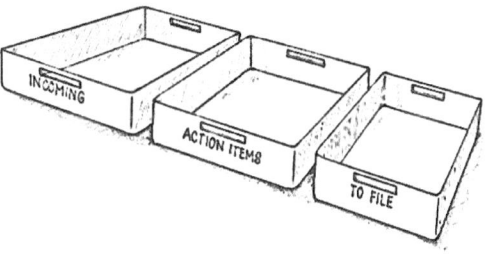 items that need action. Another basket is for items that need to be filed in my file drawer. I understand the need for keeping important papers filed, but I hate filing. So when that basket gets full, I file everything at one time. Two other baskets hold items only for my business—one for sales/marketing and another for receipts/bills.

Whether you have a separate home office, use a few drawers in the kitchen, or have a portable file box, it is important to keep this work zone separate from the other areas of your life.

One question I am often asked is how long should certain papers be kept? There is no clear-cut answer. It depends on your individual situation. Can you get the records electronically from the bank or issuing party? Would the records ever be needed? The IRS will typically go back up to three years for a personal audit, or up to six years in substantial errors. Businesses are different. My suggestion is to consult your accountant or attorney for advice.

Kid's artwork

We treasure our children's artwork. But there is too much to keep it all. To avoid getting overwhelmed, the key is proper storage and continual review and purging.

Storage can simply be one dedicated plastic storage tub or cardboard box. Or a drawer in a dresser or cabinet. For larger, flat artwork, roll several pieces together and store in a poster tube.

At the end of the school year be sure to review what has been collected, scale down to a few important pieces, and save those selected items accordingly. Involve the kids by having them pick out their favorites. Explain to them that you can't save everything. Set a limit for each, maybe one plastic bin per child. This is a good way to start them on the habit of thinking about the value of the things they save and the things they buy.

If the items are important enough to save long term, they must be stored properly. Choose an appropriately sized sturdy container. Label with the child's name and the years the artwork was created. Store this container in a safe space where it won't get damaged. To take it a step further, store the artwork so it can be easily viewed.

- For smaller flat artwork, create an art book using a binder and 8.5" x 11" plastic sleeves. Or buy an inexpensive artist portfolio. They come in sizes from 8"x11" up to 11"x17".
- For larger art or three-dimensional projects, consider taking a picture as a memory, then retire (trash) the original. You can make your own photo album or use an online service such as Shutterfly to make a photo book.
- Pick the best piece of the year, buy an inexpensive frame and hang it on the wall.

Toys, games, and other fun stuff

If you have young children, it is safe to say at least one room in your home is overrun by toys. Maybe two. The influx of new toys seems to be never ending. Birthday, holidays, special occasions. I do not have children, but I have learned from my friends that who have children there will always be some toy clutter, no matter how hard you try to clean up, or teach your children to clean up after themselves. Don't try and fight it; just do your best to keep it all from getting out of control.

I have a few strategies to help you keep the toys manageable. First, use storage containers to keep like items together. You can use large containers for big categories such as stuffed animals, dolls, cars, building blocks, or use smaller containers to categorize even further. If possible, keep the containers where the toys are used.

Second, always be reviewing and purging. As kids get older, they will outgrow some toys. If you want to save those toys for future kids, pack them away, otherwise donate, sell, or toss. Broken toys? Missing pieces? Toss. Toys they never ever play with? Donate, sell, or toss. If appropriate, get your children involved in selecting toys to donate to charity. Or do the purge when the children are sleeping to avoid arguments.

Third, gradually encourage your children to put their toys away where they belong. This will take time, and they may not always obey but the effort will be worth it. This is a great first responsibility to teach children, and it is something they can handle.

Children's books are timeless. Building a children's library at home is a great idea, especially if you have children of various ages. Like toys, children will outgrow some books. Unless they are physically damaged, books can be sold or donated.

Crafts is another big category. Paper, pencils, pens, markers, crayons, paints, glue, glitter, the list goes on and on. When organizing craft items, keep like items together and try to consolidate everything to one primary zone, ideally where the children do their arts and crafts. If that is not possible, consider using a plastic rolling cart to store the supplies and bring them to the work area during craft time. Or use a flat basket to hold currently used supplies

Books and media

Much has been said about the printed word being dead. But people bought over 600 million physical books in 2014. Even with the rise of the e-book, print books are here to stay.

When considering the value of a book, consider the information and ideas, not the paper and ink. You paid $19.99 for the latest blockbuster novel in hardcover. You read it. You enjoyed it. Now you are left with the book.

You may read it again or you may not. What is it worth? You might sell it at a yard sale for a dollar or two. You would receive the same tax deduction by donating it to a charity. Maybe you can get a few dollars more for it by selling it online. That's not a lot compared to the twenty dollars you paid for it.

Let's now consider the value you got from the book. What did you learn? How much enjoyment did you get? That is the true value of a book.

The same can be said of prerecorded music and movies. In most cases the resale value is minimal. The value is what future enjoyment you will get from listening to the music or watching the movies. Only you can decide if this value is worth the physical space the media takes up and if it fits with your vision for your space.

With media you can go all digital. For music, if you aren't attached to physical CDs, save the music to your computer or mobile device and purge the discs. Movies may be available via On Demand from your cable provider or on the internet from a site such as Netflix.

For the last few months, I have been on a mission to downsize and purge from my house things I do not need. My latest project has been my CD collection, which is huge. From a collection of many hundreds, I selected about eighty CDs I have not listened to in years and probably will never

Real Value

listen to again. I brought them to the local used record store that buys used LPs, CDs, and DVDs. I was hoping for about one dollar per disc. As I browsed the store while the clerk reviewed my collection, I realized I wouldn't get that much. Older, common CDs were selling for $1.99. They wouldn't be able to pay me one dollar and sell it for $1.99 and make enough of profit. Sure enough, the clerk called me over and said my total was $34.00. I was slightly disappointed, but only for a short time. Making money wasn't the point of this exercise. My goal was to declutter my house and create space, which I did.

If I had wanted to get more money for each CD I could have tried selling them individually on my own on eBay or Half.com. But it would have taken months, if not years, to sell them all, plus the added effort of packaging and shipping each sale. Tossing them in the trash was never an option, as they still have some value. For me selling them in bulk was the best option.

The point of this book is the value of our stuff can be determined in many ways. It is a matter of how you look at your stuff. I saw my CDs as something I once enjoyed and had gotten use of, but were now just taking up space. I also saw the value of the space I'd gain by purging. Others may see the original purchase price of twelve dollars to fifteen dollars each. This makes purging much more difficult.

This concept is not limited to books and media. It applies to everything in our homes: clothes, kitchenware, tools, electronics, toys, and collectibles, almost everything we buy. Look past the original purchase price to determine the real value.

When working with clients I coach them on how to look at their possessions. Think about the value the item currently brings you rather than the original cost. Or how much value you have received from the item over the years compared to how much you paid for it. You will start to see things differently. Look back at the chart on Page 23 in Chapter 1.

Collect for enjoyment, not profit

Do you collect something? Actually, I should ask what you collect, as I think it is safe to say most people have at least one collection. People collect things for a number of reasons. The items may be related to another interest (such as baseball cards, or movie memorabilia), or mementos of travel such as postcards, or spoons, or shot glasses). Or they collect something their parent or grandparent collected. Or perhaps they simply have a passion for the items. Coins, stamps, beer steins, cameras, typewriters, antiques, and artwork,

Real Value

the list goes on and on.

Some people collect with the hope and expectation of selling the collection and making a profit. This can be dangerous. Very few things increase in value over time. Most will decrease. Remember the Beanie Baby craze? Today most of these plush toys can be found on eBay for a fraction of the original list price. Only a few rare, early pieces are worth big bucks.

My grandmother used to collect Hummel plates and figurines. She displayed them throughout her home. Over the years I was told how valuable they were. She recently gifted me the annual collector plate for my birth year. Curious of its monetary value, I did some research and found it to be about fifteen dollars. To me the sentimental value coming from my grandmother, knowing she displayed it proudly for so many years, is worth more than that. It now hangs in my own dining room.

A train enthusiast may collect toy trains. He or she is likely to have one or more tracks set up at home to run the trains and really enjoy them. Engines and cars can be swapped out every so often on the running lines.

You should collect something because it brings you joy. You should be able to enjoy your collection on a daily basis. For over thirty years, my friend Betty collected Barbie dolls. Not just any Barbie dolls, but the expensive, premium, collector's item editions. She kept them in the original boxes, packed away in her basement. If she wanted to display a particular doll in her home, she bought a duplicate. She recently moved across the country to a smaller house and ended up selling her entire collection to someone at a substantial loss. I know she enjoyed the process of collecting

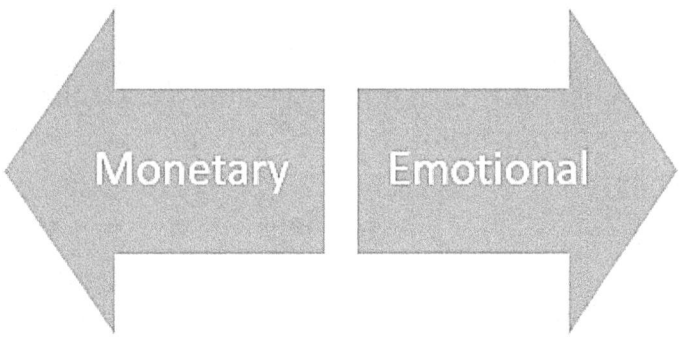

over the years, and the thrill of each new purchase. I can definitely relate to that. After the acquisition, though, nothing. The majority of the dolls were packed away. She was collecting strictly as an investment. By her estimate, over the years she paid well over $20,000, and only got back $3,000.

Betty may have recovered more money had she individually sold each doll herself, but that would have taken time, something she did not have. Collecting as an investment can work, if you do the research, choose the right collectible, and are able to sell at the most profitable time. Those are big ifs. It is much safer to collect for enjoyment. That way the real value of the collection will be guaranteed.

Hobbies

We all have hobbies and interests outside of our work, which vary greatly from person to person. Maybe you like arts and crafts. Or doing home improvements. Or cooking is your thing and you obsess over cookbooks and kitchen gadgets. Or staying active through team sports and exercise. Or you are an outdoors person who enjoys camping, hiking, or fishing and all the gear that goes with it. Whether you have a hobby in which you are creating something or doing something, hobbies generally come with stuff, and if you are passionate about your hobby, the amount of stuff can soon become out of hand. What if you have more than one hobby? The potential for clutter is there if limits are not set.

It all comes back to your vision and what you value. Set limits on how much space you will allow for each hobby.

First, identify your active hobbies. What do you really enjoy and spend time doing? Decide how many active hobbies are reasonable. Do they fit in with your vision?

Do you have past hobbies, or hobbies you planned to spend time on but never did? Be honest with yourself as to whether these fit in your vision for your life going forward. Letting go is ok.

What are your hobbies?

Painting	Collecting
Arts & Crafts	Music
Knitting	Watching Sports
Photography	Reading
Running	Pets
Weight Training	Computers
Hiking	Puzzles & Games
Camping	Jewelry
Fishing	Antiques
Golf	Cooking
Tennis	History
Bowling	Writing
Team Sports	Science
Gardening	

Perhaps you really enjoyed scrapbooking ten years ago, but now you would rather spend your time reading. Make a plan for your scrapbooking

Real Value

supplies. Or maybe you always wanted to take up painting. You bought all the supplies, dedicated a corner of the basement as a studio, but have yet to pick up a brush. You are just too busy with work and family and other hobbies right now. Realistically, do you see yourself painting in the next year? Would that basement space be better used right now? Either commit to the hobby, or pack up the supplies for use in the future, or make a plan to sell or donate them. If you pack them up, give yourself another review date. Say in two years, if you haven't painted, you'll donate the items.

What items in your home are associated with your hobbies, whether actively or passively?

Are the items organized effectively to allow you to enjoy your hobby?

Are the items affecting other areas of your life negatively?

Once you have identified your active hobbies one by one, process the corresponding supplies and determine using the sort, review, organize, and purge techniques. Dedicate a work zone. Keep in mind how much physical space you have for this hobby.

Seasonal items

We all have items used only a certain time of the year: decorations, outdoor furniture, barbeque equipment, party supplies, pool accessories, sports equipment, etc. Some may be related to the hobbies we just discussed. Others may be used for specific holidays or seasons. When not in use, these items are packed away until next year. The end of the season is a great time to sort, review, and purge before you pack everything away.

Think about the last holiday you decorated the house. Did you buy new decorations this year? Have you not used certain ones in a few years? Is something out of style? Broken? When the season was over and the decorations came down, did you immediately pack everything away or take a few minutes to review? The end of a season is the ideal time to purge unused items and downsize your inventory to what you actually use, instead of packing everything way with the intent to deal with it next year. By doing so you will immediately gain some storage space and make decorating next year much easier since you won't have to sort through unused items to find what you really need. If you need to replace anything, you can plan accordingly, whether it is to take advantage of an after season clearance sale or shop off-season instead of waiting until next year when everything will be full price.

Long-term storage

Think about your current home. How many

storage spots do you have that you rarely access? The attic, the basement, the back of the garage, and the closet in the guest room. Do you know what is in there? Did you put something there with the intention of dealing with it later, only now it is five years later and the item is buried under a mountain of other "to deal with later" items? Are the boxes and bins clearly labeled? Are the boxes and bins still in good condition, protecting the contents?

Are you paying for off-site storage? How long have you had the storage unit? Off-site storage should be used as a temporary solution to a short-term situation. Unfortunately, most people use it as long-term storage with no game plan. If you are currently paying for off-site storage, calculate how much you have spent so far, and the annual cost. Then estimate how much the stuff you are storing is worth. A relative of mine had a storage unit for over ten years to store some furniture, a washer and dryer, and other personal items. At a conservative fifty a month, over the course of ten years, she spent $6,000 on storage fees. I doubt the furniture and appliances were worth that when they went into storage. Ten years later, I'd be surprised if they had any real value.

Long-term storage should not mean forever storage, never to be dealt with again. When you put something in long-term storage, make sure the item is clearly and accurately labeled. Make sure the box or bin is appropriate for the item and the location. Make notes on what is being stored and where. See the upcoming section on general home organization for details on that last tip.

Moving and downsizing: plan ahead

The average American moves once every five years and 11 times over his or her lifetime. Although in the last ten years, the move rate has dropped, partly due to our aging population.

At some point, you may downsize. Why? You no longer need as much space. Or you want to save money. Or you desire less home maintenance. Or you need to move into assisted living or a care facility. No matter what the reason, the reality is you will have less space for your stuff. We tend to accumulate a lot of stuff over the years packed away in closets and basements and attics. This section focuses on downsizing, but even if you are moving into a similar sized home, many of the suggestions still apply. All homes, even if they have approximately the same square footage, have different shapes and sizes of rooms, different number of closets, and more or less built-in storage space. If you are moving from one part of the country to another, or even from one neighborhood to another, you may find yourself living differently. Did you have a home near a lake or the ocean and now are moving a few hours away from water? Are you moving from the north to the south? Are you moving from a home with a large outdoor patio to a city townhouse? Each home "lives" differently. You may no longer need that beach equipment, or the winter coats, or the large grill.

It is important to plan ahead. You will save time and money, the move will be less stressful, and you will be comfortable in your new home faster if you get rid of things you know you will not need before you move. By planning ahead you can hopefully keep the same standard of living and comfort. When we have to act quickly or respond to an emergency, sacrifices are usually made.

As you plan your move, ask yourself what do you really need? You want your new space to feel like home. If you have been in your current home for many years, there may be some sadness in moving. Having the new space feel like the old space will help lessen the emotions.

Maximize your new space. Take measurements, determine if your existing furniture will fit. What will be excess? What available storage will you have? You may need some pieces that do double duty, such as a storage bench or ottoman that can not only act as seating, but hold useful items, too.

Bring only what you truly need and love. We

talked about how people use twenty percent of their possessions eighty percent of the time. The rest mostly goes unused.

Allow time to rehome what you do not need: give to family members, sell or donate, trash what is left. When you have time, you can get top dollar for items you want to sell. If you have less time, you may want to take items to Goodwill, the Salvation Army, or another local charity and receive a tax deduction for the donations. When you have to act quickly, you may need to take whatever money you can get, or throw valuable items in the trash. See Chapter 7 for more ideas on what to do with unneeded items.

The less you have to move, the less it costs to move. Most moving companies charge by weight, volume, or number of boxes. It will also take less time and less stress to unpack, and you will feel settled in your new home more quickly.

Anytime you can plan ahead and prepare for such an important, large event, you will be more successful than if facing an emergency situation, under time constraints and stress. Try to avoid moving everything you have into the new space without first sorting and purging and then trying to figure it all out once you are in the new space. It will take much longer, you won't have any breathing room, and you will be living with extra furniture and boxes: a stressful situation. By not purging and sorting before the move, you might be tempted to keep your possessions in boxes in the garage or in a storage unit where you are unable to use them.

I have moved three times since I graduated from college. The last move was from a small one bedroom apartment into a three bedroom house. My family and friends helped me move, and they were amazed at how much stuff I had stored in my small apartment. My place did not look cluttered or cramped as I had maximized the space, and taken advantage of every storage opportunity.

Upon moving into the new larger home, I managed to fill every room and the basement of my new house with my existing stuff. Much of it had been in boxes and bins—things I had collected and saved over the years. Seeing everything out in the open made me think twice about all of it. Did I really need it? I was motivated to start downsizing my possessions, even though I now had the space for it all.

Considerations for seniors and elderly

As discussed in the last section, many of us will downsize our homes as we age. Some of us, if financially and physically able, may stay in our homes long term. In the senior care industry, this is called "aging in place." In either scenario, as we get older our needs change. Getting organized can help ensure that we have a safe and functional living environment.

Consider senior mobility and safety. You can easily navigate your home now. But what if you had to use a walker or a wheelchair? The pathways may need to be wider and free of clutter. Similarly, you currently have no problem reaching items on the top shelf of the kitchen cabinets, but that may not always be the case. Items used regularly need to be stored not too high or too low so they are easily accessible. As we age, our needs change. Our organization plans need to change as well.

As I mentioned in the last section, having the new space feel like the old space will help lessen the any emotions that arise from moving. This is especially important with seniors who may be more vulnerable, from dealing with the loss of a spouse or a new medical condition, or having to give up some personal freedom.

General home organization

I encourage you to become organized one room at a time, thinking about work zones. When everything has a home, clutter will less likely occur. In some cases, though, we have to think of the home as a whole. Here are a few more tips to help in that area.

We all have countless manuals and instruction booklets and warranties for items in the home.

Appliances, electronics, major home improvements. How do you keep them organized?

1. Get two standard 3-ring binders and fill with 8.5" x 11" plastic protector sleeves.
2. Gather all the manuals and instruction booklets and warranties for items in the house.
3. Use one binder for all major appliances and built-in fixtures—anything that would stay with the home if you sold it.
4. Use the other binder for smaller appliances that you will take with you when you move, such as electronics, garden equipment, etc.
5. For each manual or booklet, write the date of purchase, store of purchase, and price. Slide it into its own plastic sleeve.

Now everything is stored in one place and is easily accessible when needed. If you do not want to use binders, two shoe boxes work as well or any other container. As long as everything is together in one place.

Another idea for organizing your home is creating a house map. Using any standard notebook, give each room of the house a page. On each page, list the items stored in that room, including the ones not visible or obvious. For example, what is in the attic versus the basement? Where are the extra batteries? Where is the air mattress? Where are the large platters that are only use at Thanksgiving? If you organized your house in logical work zones, this step may be unnecessary, but taking a few minutes to take some notes may save you hours months from now when you are looking for that random item.

Throughout this book, I talk about downsizing and only keeping what you need. But in some cases, duplicates make sense. Frequently used items could be kept in every room, so they are readily available when needed. For example, keeping a flashlight in every room or at least every floor of the house in case of emergency makes sense. A pair of reading glasses in the living room where you read, and one at your desk where you pay bills, and keep another pair in your purse. Think about the small items you use on a regular basis in multiple rooms. Scissors, a notepad, pencils, and pens are a few examples.

Chapter 7
What comes next?

What to do with extra stuff

As you organize your home, you will undoubtedly identify items you no longer want or need. Please don't just move everything to the garage or basement, or even worse default to blindly throwing the items out. Your options will depend upon the actual item, but here are some suggestions.

You may be able to rehome the item to family and friends. This is especially important if you want to keep heirlooms or memorabilia in the family. Or perhaps you know a college graduate or newlyweds starting a new home. Social media is a great way to spread the word when you have items to rehome.

If the item is monetarily valuable, consider selling it. Selling what we do not need is a great way to raise money to pay off credit card debt, save for emergencies, or put toward a special purchase or vacation. You have many options. I've listed the most popular below, with some pros and cons. Keep in mind everything is relative to your own situation. The time and effort involved in selling may not be worth the return

- Craigslist – Local classified ads online. What did we do before Craigslist? Oh yes, we placed a small advertisement in the newspaper, which used abbreviations, cost money, and ran for a limited number of days.
Pro: Craigslist is easy to use and free. You can post pictures, as well as modify text and selling price as needed. Many items will sell quickly.
Con: Unless you meet at a public place, potential buyers are coming to your house. This may not appeal to you for privacy or security concerns. Also, dealing with potential buyers can be a hassle.

- Facebook – Facebook has local virtual yard sale groups. You post a picture of an item with a description and price. Anyone in the group interested will contact you. This option is

Real Value

similar to Craigslist, with the same pros and cons. The added benefit is you are targeting local buyers who are interested in used goods.

- eBay – eBay has been a blessing and a curse for selling your possessions. You can sell pretty much anything to anyone anywhere, but this convenience and reach has brought down the value of some collectibles that were previously hard to come by.
Pro: You can reach a wider audience, and bidding can increase profits. eBay is great for collectibles or other items with a specific target sales market, and for items that are easy to ship.
Con: Dealing with packing and shipping can be a hassle. Also, eBay does charge minor listing and sales fees.

- SWAP.com – This site is an online consignment shop for children's items and women's clothing. You send the company a box of items, they process and post for sale on their website. As items are sold, they handle shipping and collect payments and send you the proceeds, minus reasonable fees.
Pro: Less work on your part than eBay.
Con: Some items may not sell, in which case you can pay to have them shipped back or you have the company donate them for you.

- Yard Sales / Garage Sales – Someone may want what you no longer need. A yard sale is an easy, quick way to clear away the items you have purged, and make some money in the process.
  Pro: Sell everything in a day or two. Little out of pocket costs. Worthwhile if you have many items to sell and live in an area where you will get potential buyers to stop by.
  Con: Yard sales can be a lot of work for minimal profit. Most items will sell for very little, usually a quarter of the original purchase price, even less for books, media, and clothes. Consider what you have available for sale and what your overall profit might be.

- Estate Sales – Let a professional sell your stuff in your own home. They are the experts in how to market and stage the sale and how to price your items for top dollar. Estate sales are commonly used before a move or when you have many rooms of items to sell.
  Pro: You can sell most everything in a day or two, letting others do the work.
  Con: Potential buyers will be walking around your home looking at items for sale. Estate sale companies typically charge around thirty percent of proceeds plus advertising costs as a

fee. Be sure you understand the terms of any agreement before signing a contract.

- Auctions – Let a professional sell your stuff at their location. Auction houses bring buyers together to bid on your items. Contrary to popular belief, auction houses sell more than high priced art and antiques. Many auction houses will sell anything—with some obvious exceptions—someone else will buy.
  Pro: The auction company will typically advertise your items in advance, to their known list of potential buyers. They will do all the work.
  Con: They will charge a fee. Based on their experience, they will only take items they know will sell. You will be on your own for anything else.

- Online auctions – These are a relatively new option: a hybrid of regular auctions, Craigslist, and eBay. You take pictures and provide information, the company sets up your auction on a website. They handle the auction and payments. Buyers come to you on a specific predetermined date for pickup.
  Pro: The fees are lower than regular auctions or estate sales. An online auction has a potentially wider audience than a live in-person auction.

Con: You have to do some of the work. Buyers may be hesitant to buy certain items from only a picture or two.

If money is not a concern, or you do not want to go through the hassle of selling, you can donate many items to charity. Most charities will take clothing, furniture, small appliances, and toys, and some will pick up directly from your home. When donating items to charity consider whether someone else might want the items. Stained or torn clothing, broken furniture, or appliances are no good to anyone. Many charities end up trashing a good deal of donated items because they are too damaged. This ends up costing the charity money.

Sheets and towels not suitable for charity can be donated to animal shelters or animal rescue groups for use as bedding for homeless animals. These organizations usually have limited financial resources and rely on donated items to meet their needs.

If you cannot sell or give it away, see if you can recycle the item. We all know about the basic

Real Value

things to recycle: paper, plastic, bottles, and cans. What you may not know is not all plastic is recyclable, and many other types of items can be recycled.

When recycling paper consider what should first be shredded to prevent identify theft. If you do not have a home shredder, there are companies who will shred paper for a nominal fee. Many municipalities or local organizations sponsor shredding truck days.

Clothing and textiles that are no longer usable can also be recycled. Some charities will take these items and then sell them to a third party that will make use of them. Or you may be able to donate to such a company directly. Many of large metal bins you see in parking lots that ask for donations are managed by for-profit companies that will recycle the clothing. While not supporting a charity, this option is better than having the items end up in a landfill. Read the signs on the bins before you donate.

Most electronics are recyclable, and in some communities cannot be put out with general trash. Similarly hazardous waste also must be disposed of properly to protect the environment. Regulations vary, so it is best to check with your local authorities for the rules in your area.

If you aren't sure if something can be recycled, perform an internet search. There are many sites, such as Earth911.com, that will educate you on how to recycle responsibly. The rules on what can and cannot be recycled are ever changing. You may even find an option in your local area.

Lastly, some items do belong in the trash. They have served their purpose, lived out their usefulness, and now must be disposed of. Regulations on what you can dispose of locally will vary; check with your municipality. If you have large items to dispose of, there are many national junk services available, such as CollegeHunks.com or 1800GOTJUNK.com.

See the Appendix for a complete list of resources for all topics in this section.

Maintain, and modify if needed

New habits will take time to become part of your everyday routine. This small investment in the short term will reap great benefits in the long run.

For each room or work zone, decide what an appropriate maintenance schedule should be. For the kitchen, you may want to clear the clutter every day but review the pantry once a week before grocery shopping. For your home office, once a week might be sufficient. Every season you will review your wardrobe looking for items to toss. You are in control and can best decide what works for you.

Create a lost and found box and put it in a central location of your home, maybe a hallway or the living room or kitchen. If you find something out of place, put it in the box. Then every day or once a week take the box around the house and put things back where they belong. Get the family involved, and have everyone check the box for items that belong to them.

Set up ground rules for bringing new items into the home. If part of your organizing plan was to limit items to what fits in your current space, if you bring in something new, you may decide to purge something old. One in, one out. Again, decide what works for you.

If a system doesn't seem to work for you, do not be afraid to change it. If you fall back into old patterns, do not give up. Take a step back to review where you strayed from your plan. Make small changes to get back on track. You did it once, you can do it again.

Mental clutter

You've cleared the physical clutter and organized your home—or at least started. How about clearing the clutter from your mind? One tip I give my clients, which seems very simple but can have a great impact, is to write everything down in a notebook. That way you don't have to think about it all the time. Release it from your brain.

You don't need to worry about forgetting something important. Simply reference your notebook as needed daily or weekly to plan your time. Lists are great, but how often do you write a note or list on a slip of paper and then misplace the paper? Or your desk or counter becomes covered in small slips? Use one notebook to keep everything in one place. Or if you have a smart phone, there are many note taking apps available.

With a clear mind, you can focus on what is most important. You can spend your time on the task at hand, not on what you need to do later or tomorrow. If you'd like to pursue this area further, there are many great books on time management and personal productivity.

Why a professional organizer?

A professional organizer can help you set realistic goals and define an action plan to achieve those goals. He or she will act as coach and mentor, guiding you in the process of getting organized.

Working with a professional organizer, you will be more than twice as productive as if you were working alone. The professional organizer will keep you motivated and accountable and support you in your journey to achieving your goals.

A professional organizer brings fresh ideas and

experience to your project, offering best practices, tips, and tricks. He or she also offers an independent voice.

Finally, a professional organizer will help you save you time and money in the long run. Yes, there is a cost associated to hiring someone, but as we have discussed in this book, we need to consider the value you will get in return. The monetary cost should be compared to the time and money you will save over the months and years ahead.

Additional help and ideas

I hope this book has shown you and new ways to look at your time, your space and your stuff, and given you the tools and techniques to become organized. This book is only the start of your journey to getting organized and staying organized. There are tons of ideas and inspiration out there waiting for you. Read other organizing books on specific topics of interest to you or follow professional organizer blogs for quick tips and tricks. Watch television programs on organizing to keep you motivated. Check out Pinterest boards for inspiration and ideas.

Do not forget your friends, family, and coworkers. Share your journey with them. They may have some advice to share, or want to take the journey with you.

Appendix

Note: URLs change over time. These lists will be kept current and expanded on www.RealValueTheBook.com

What to do with your unneeded stuff

Selling options

Craigslist.org – Online, local classified ads

eBay.com – Online marketplace to sell just about anything

Half.com – Part of eBay, but focuses solely on the sale of books, CDs, and DVDs. The inventory system allows you to list items based on UPC code and immediately see for how much others are selling the same item.

Amazon.com – They will buy back certain books for site credit.

SWAP.com – Online consignment shop for women's and children's items.

Maxsold.com – Online auction site

Donating options

Freecycle.org – A collection of local groups that

give and get stuff free in their own towns. Using an email distribution list, members post items they are giving away. The organization is nonprofit and strives to keep worthy items out of landfills.

Charities with donation drop off locations:
Dress For Success – Provides clothing to women returning to the workforce
http://DressForSuccess.org

Goodwill – Local thrift stores
http://www.goodwill.org/

Lions Club – Eye Glasses
http://www.lionsclubs.org/EN/how-we-serve/health/sight/eyeglass-recycling.php

These charities will pick up donations at your home:
Vietnam Veterans of America
http://www.pickupplease.org/

Military Order of the Purple Heart
http://www.purpleheartpickup.org/

Lupus Foundation of America
http://www.lupuspickup.org/

The Salvation Army
https://satruck.org/

Recycling info
Natural Resources Defense Council
http://www.nrdc.org/recycling/

Earth911
http://www.earth911.com/

Dispose My Meds
http://www.disposemymeds.org/

Stopping junk at the source
DMA Choice – Reference site for getting off postal mailing lists
https://www.dmachoice.org/

US Do Not Call registry
https://www.donotcall.gov/

Donation monetary value
US IRS tax deductions website
https://www.irs.gov/publications/p561/ar02.html

Good Will Donation Valuation Guide
https://www.goodwill.org/wp-content/uploads/2010/12/Donation_Valuation_Guide.pdf

Salvation Army Donation Value Guide
https://satruck.org/Home/DonationValueGuide

What are your collectibles worth?

Online resources and price guides can give you a general idea if your collectibles have any monetary valuable, or are mainly sentimental in value. If you have something potentially valuable, then you can seek out an expert opinion.

Kovels – General Antiques
http://www.kovels.com/

Beckett – Sports and Collectibles
http://www.beckett.com/price-guides

Replacements.com – Online buyer and seller of china, crystal, silver, and collectibles.
http://www.replacements.com/

PCGS – Price guide for coins
http://www.pcgs.com/prices/

Whitman – Price guide for coins
https://www.whitman.com/coin-values/collectible-us-coins-introduction/

Collectors Corner – Marketplace for coins, currency, cards, and stamps
http://www.collectorscorner.com

Where to get organizing ideas?

Pinterest.com – A social media site where users post pictures and videos of their hobbies and interests
http://www.Pinterest.com

Real Simple – A monthly home and lifestyle magazine and website that features decorating and organizing ideas and tips
www.realsimple.com

Getting Organized Magazine – An online source for organizing ideas
http://www.gettingorganizedmagazine.com/

HGTV – Cable television channel and associated website focused on home and garden design Features shows and articles on organizing.
http://www.hgtv.com

Finding a professional organizer
www.NAPO.net
www.FindMyOrganizer.com
www.HomeAdvisor.com
www.AngiesList.com
Your local Chamber of Commerce

Acknowledgements

I would like to thank the following people, without whose support my professional organizing business and this book would not have been possible.

Thank you to my family for supporting my decision to change careers and follow my passion: Bill & Chris Odalen, Matthew Odalen & Mara Kennedy, Chrissy Odalen & Sean Kearns, Sherry & Tony Ardito.

Thank you to those who were so generous with their advice when I first started my organizing business: Brian Blatz, Tom Callahan, and David Leta.

Thank you to Adam Sullens, an amazing graphic artist, for all his hard work, and for putting up with my constant change requests.

Thank you to Leena Thakar-Bagawde for her delightful illustrations in this book.

Lastly, thank you to my editor and publisher, Karen Hodges Miller for helping me find my writing voice and turn an idea and a dream into this book.

About the author

Professional organizer John Odalen is a detail-oriented professional with a natural talent for organizing and an inherent need for order. John spent twenty years in the software industry focusing on customer success, quality assurance, and project management before transferring these skills to his new business, Organize and Maintain. John specializes in helping people who feel overwhelmed and do not know where to start. He helps his clients create a vision and define and achieve their goals while also coaching them on how to get organized and stay organized.

An animal lover, John has volunteered with various animal rescue organizations where he lives, and has fostered dozens of kittens and cats, adopting five hard to place cats himself. Currently, John volunteers with The English School at LRPC, an English as a Second Language school for adults. In his spare time, he enjoys cooking, gardening, and exercising and watches way too much television.

He is a member of the National Association of Professional Organizers (NAPO) and is also a Certified Scrum Master (CSM) and a Certified Associate in Project Management (CAPM).

Born and raised in New Jersey, John currently lives in Lawrenceville, New Jersey with his dog Travis. His book on organizing, *Real Value: New Ways to Think About Your Time, Your Space & Your Stuff,* published in 2016 by Open Door Publications, offers a fresh way to look at organizing your home or business. John is available for speaking engagements and is accepting new organizing clients in central New Jersey and the surrounding areas.

www.OrganizeAndMaintain.com

www.ingramcontent.com/pod-product-compliance
Lightning Source LLC
LaVergne TN
LVHW021359080426
835508LV00020B/2351